Fashion Industry and Social Media
Influencing Trends

Table of Contents

In order to be irreplaceable one must always be different.

— Coco Chanel

Chapter 1. Introduction

In an exciting new era where haute couture meets high tech, this Special Report delves profoundly into the extraordinary synergy between the Fashion Industry and Social Media. We explore their dynamic interplay and dissect how they're not just tracking but setting the pace in determining what's 'in' and what's 'next'. With engaging stories, expert insights and intricate analyses, this report artfully unravels how Facebook posts, Instagram hashtags, and TikTok streams are, quite literally, shaping the cut of our clothes. So, whether you're a fashion lover, influencer, designer, or simply curious about the digital revolution transforming the runway, our meticulously crafted report is your golden ticket, serving up a front row seat to this headline-grabbing spectacle. Let's inspire, inform, and invigorate your viewpoint, all the while capturing the movement of trends from the catwalk to the keyboard, and then straight into our wardrobes. Indulge in this intriguing saga and let us fashion your understanding of this vibrant, viral vista!

Chapter 2. The Fashion Industry: A Snapshot

In a brilliant display of creativity and commerce, the fashion industry has continually made its mark as one of the most vibrant sectors of global economic advancement. Acknowledging universally its significant place in painting a nation's economic canvas, this sector has been marked by its constant odyssey towards new fashion ideologies, business models, and technological integrations, providing a brilliant kaleidoscope of ingenuity and innovation.

2.1. The Landscape of the Fashion Industry

The fashion industry, with its inherent complexity, is a vast, multifaceted realm that extends beyond haute couture or high-end fashion. It encompasses everything from affordable fast-fashion behemoths to independent designers struggling to carve a niche for themselves in the volatile and often highly competitive marketplace. Beyond that, an increasingly critical element of the fashion industry is sustainability and how various players, large and small, are incorporating responsible practices into their operation.

In its simplest interpretation, the fashion industry involves the manufacturing and marketing of clothing and accessories. However, when delved deeper into the industry's trenches, it becomes unmistakably clear that this simple description belies an intricate global network consisting of fashion designers, textile producers, manufacturing units, retail outlets, marketing professionals, fashion journalists and critics, models, event organizers, among numerous others. Each of these individual nodes undeniably adds to the colossal tapestry that the industry composes.

2.2. The Economic Impact of the Fashion Industry

The fashion industry is a colossal engine for global economy, with a value of approximately 3 trillion USD, which equates to roughly 2% of the world's total economic output. It is significant not just because of its sheer magnitude, but also due to the countless other industries it influences and intersects with, like textile manufacturing and retail, to name just a few.

Moreover, it also contributes enormously to employment worldwide. According to the World Economic Forum, it employs over 60 million people along its dense value chain, thus acting as an economic lifeline for countless families globally.

2.3. The Evolution of the Fashion Industry

Looking back at the historical tapestry of the fashion industry, it's evident that it has evolved dramatically over time, corresponding to a range of external influences, including cultural shifts, technological innovations, political events, and of course, the advent of social media. As the world has grown increasingly interconnected, the fashion industry's trajectory has also skated towards a global perspective, transforming from local cottage industries to international fashion weeks.

The industry continues to evolve, marked by notable milestones such as the introduction of ready-to-wear clothing in the 1960s and the dawn of fast-fashion in the 2000s. With each turn, the industry becomes more responsive, democratic, and accessible.

2.4. The Challenges and Opportunities for the Fashion Industry

However, the journey has not been without its fair share of challenges. Issues like unethical labor practices, environmental sustainability, body positivity, diversity, and inclusivity have seen rising debates within the industry.

Yet, along with these challenges, the fashion industry presents numerous opportunities. The sustainability movement has given rise to a burgeoning trend of 'slow fashion'. Inclusivity, once an overlooked necessity, is now at the forefront of many fashion campaigns, leading to an industry that is more diverse than ever.

Technology too has been a key player in the evolution of the industry. With innovations in e-commerce and digital marketing, the reach of fashion brands is no longer limited by geographical boundaries. More recently, the incorporation of social media has changed the rhythm of the fashion industry at its core, an indication of further transformations to come.

In conclusion, the fashion industry is a vibrant, ever-evolving, and complex landscape, marked by ceaseless innovation and constant progress, yet challenged by issues of sustainability and inclusivity. The dynamic dialogues that continue to shape the industry are indications of the endless possibilities that coat the future of fashion. With the emergence of platforms such as social media, the industry is set to traverse new horizons, embracing and redefining the narratives that fashion etches on the global canvas. Indeed, the snapshot of the fashion industry is nothing short of a panoramic capture of vivacity, ingenuity, controversy, tradition, evolution, and most importantly, a promise of continual metamorphosis.

Chapter 3. Social Media: The New Vogue

The ultimate revolution in our epoch is indisputably the advent of social media, which has perceivably shaken up numerous conventional structures of commerce, information, communication, and none so much as in the sphere of the fashion industry. In this virtual realm of hashtags, likes, and shares, fashion has found a new modus operandi to not only showcase but evolve its designs, trends, and styles, with a fervor that has briskly surpassed time-honored media like printed glossy magazines and fashion talks on televised networks.

3.1. The Reimagining of a Platform: Social Media in Fashion

The influence of social media on fashion lies in its ability to redefine the traditional conduits of information exchange and commerce. Where once fashionable trends were the preserve of a select circle of designers, runways, models, and glossy print publication, today, the narratives of style and trends are as diversified and democratized as the broad spectrum of social media users themselves.

Fashion has always prospered on the currency of 'newness', in its quest to persistently redefine what is 'in vogue'. This aspect aligns flawlessly with the essence of social media platforms, which thrive on the constant churn of refreshed content - new images, videos, 'viral' trends, and memes, steered by the choices and preferences of its users.

3.2. The Social Media Landscape: Where Fashion Meets Virality

When discussing the vogue of social media within fashion, it is crucial to understand the distinct ecosystems within the vast world of virtual networks. Each platform caters to a specific user demographic, functionality, and content format, and thus, influences the conception and diffusion of fashion trends differently.

Facebook, for instance, with its ultimate feature of forming 'Groups' has permitted the creation of many fashion communities, where users can share their fashion ideas, new buys, or seek style advice. Instagram, on the other hand, has been life-changing for the fashion industry. Its image-centric functionality perfectly serves the visual nature of fashion, where a mere image of model strutting a designer's new collection, or an influencer posing in a trendy ensemble, can inspire millions of followers to rush to stores, both online and physical, to mimic the look.

Micro-blogs like Twitter allow for real-time feedback on fashion shows, trends, and faux pas, encouraging a vibrant discourse, while Snapchat offers ephemeral 'sneak-peeks' into the behind-the-scenes of fashion houses or the daily wardrobes of fashion-forward individuals. Pinterest works as a veritable style inspiration board, where users gather and share clothing and accessory 'pins' to help craft their look. And the latest hotbed of viral fashion content, TikTok, with its short, impactful videos, is fostering a new generation of DIY fashion, quick style hacks, and discount shopping hauls.

3.3. The Transcendence of Fashion: Micro-influencers and User-Generated Content

A notable repercussion of this intersection of fashion and social media has been the ascension of the 'Influencer.' From celebrities to self-made Instagram personalities, these individuals wield considerable authority, shaping sartorial choices for a vast audience. Here, authenticity is key; as their followers often perceive these influencers as ordinary people, their recommendations are often considered genuine and relatable.

Where once fashion was top-down, with designers and fashion houses dictating the trends, today, under the influence of social media, it has become largely democratized. User-generated content, significantly, has changed the game. With an abundance of DIY videos, outfit-of-the-day posts, and hashtags like #streetstyle, everyday users are increasingly becoming the trendsetters!

3.4. The Dark Underbelly: Negative Impacts and The Fast Fashion Conundrum

While the influence of social media on fashion has indeed been transformative, it is vital to consider its potentially damaging effects. The constant craving for novelty fueled by social media platforms and influencers can lead to overconsumption and wastage, giving rise to the fast-fashion crisis. More so, the loss of personal data privacy, online harassment, and unrealistic beauty standards are other critical concerns.

3.5. Conclusion: An Unstoppable Force in Fashion

In conclusion, social media has become the new vogue, forging fresh pathways for the fashion industry, from trendsetting to marketing and retailing. Despite challenges, its influence is only set to grow, driven by the proliferation of digital tech and the continual evolution of social media platforms. Despite the myriad concerns, we cannot overlook the novel opportunities it presents to artfully craft our style narratives, build communities, pioneer new fashion ideas, and drive a more sustainable, inclusive future. Be it as a participant or spectator, in this era of social media; everyone gets to have their fashion moment in the spotlight.

Chapter 4. The Confluence of Fashion and Social Media

In the ushering whirlwind of the information age, the intersection of fashion and social media represents an intriguing focal point, a veritable confluence where the traditional meets the avant-garde. This intersection has given birth to a never-before-experienced dynamism, blending the vivacity of change with the solidity drawn from the annals of fashion history. Together, these tactical collisions thereby craft a compelling panorama of style ephemerality, consumer behavior, style reinterpretation, and fashion-forward propulsion.

4.1. The Symbiotic Relationship

The profound bond between fashion and social media unfolds as no less than a symbiotic companionship. The former, a historically transformative force, has consistently revamped itself, absorbing swayed societal currents and mirroring them through vibrant fabrics and poignant styles. The latter, a 21st-century marvel, has transformed everyone into a digital native, connecting people across geographical boundaries and disseminating information at breakneck speed.

The genesis of this symbiosis lies in the reciprocal nature of their relationship. Social media platforms act as megaphones, amplifying trends set by mainstream fashion. Simultaneously, feedback from millions of users directs fashion's evolution, moulding its trajectory with an unmistakable precision that lies exquisitely in real-time reaction and reception.

While social media offers the fashion industry an unparalleled platform to reach the global audience, the fashion industry reciprocates by providing engaging content that drives user interactions across multiple platforms. It's a relationship of give-and-take, where both entities flourish symbiotically.

4.2. The Catapult Effect

The seemingly insurmountable distance between couture houses and common consumers has dramatically collapsed with the advent of social media platforms. Increasing transparency, these platforms negate the hierarchical barriers that traditionally shrouded fashion, bringing the glitz and glamour right into our palm-held screens.

This escalation of accessibility underpins the catapult effect social media has had on the fashion industry. Now, consumers are not passive receptors of trends handed down to them; instead, they actively participate in trend creation, contributing their unique perspectives through 'likes', 'shares', and 'comments'. This, in turn, furnishes the concoction of trend democracy. From fast fashion brands to luxury fashion labels, every participant listens keenly to the consumer's voice, enabling them to tailor their collections with an agility hitherto unseen.

4.3. Feeding the Fast Fashion Phenomenon

An important subsidiary narrative within this broader saga is the rise and reign of fast fashion. A term decked out in mixed reviews, fast fashion refers to inexpensive clothing produced rapidly by mass-market retailers in response to the latest trends. And the fuel for this speed? Social media.

By compressively collapsing the runway to retail timeframe, social media has became an accelerant for the fast fashion phenomenon. Brands like H&M, Zara, and ASOS leverage the power of instant communication to track the latest trends from global fashion weeks and translate them into wearable, affordable pieces at lightning-quick speed. Furthermore, the excitement generated around these quickly changing trends encourages the continual refresh of wardrobe, fuelling the cyclic nature of fast fashion.

4.4. Influencers: The New-age Couturiers

No conversation about the nexus between fashion and social media is complete without the mention of a major player – Influencers. These digital trendsetters are the nexus between consumers and brands, often serving as human billboards that showcase fashion products. Instagram, with its visually appealing interface, rules the roost in this respect.

From micro-influencers with a modest number of dedicated followers to macro-influencers boasting millions, these individuals hold striking power in the fashion industry. Brands formally partner with influencers who align with their image, creating a curated blend of aspirational lifestyle content straddling between accessibility and likened exclusivity. This bridge once again underscores the crucial role social media plays in fashion, systematically rewriting the rulebook by which the industry has played for decades.

As we continue to voyage through the ceaselessly evolving landscape of fashion and social media, the dynamics of this confluence promise an exciting ensemble of challenges and opportunities. The power to stir, mold, and rupture long-standing norms resides within this digital liaison, dauntlessly stimulating the ethos of a sartorial revolution, ongoing and relentless.

If the pens of fashion critics were mightier than swords, the fingertips of the digital native are the conductors of fashion's present symphony. With every scroll, click, and share, the boundaries of the industry are redrawn, making the confluence of fashion and social media, an arena of towering potential and electrifying curiosity. It's certainly not a stretch to proclaim that the future of fashion lies in our digital hands. And for that, the fabric of the industry must weave in social media, or risk being left threadbare.

Chapter 5. From Catwalks to Instagram: The Digital Revolution

The digital revolution's impact on the fashion industry has been monumental. The once exclusive domain, ruled by high-end designers and fashion moguls, has been democratized by the advent of social media platforms, particularly Instagram. Today, the transference of trends from the catwalk to Instagram is almost instantaneous, closing space-time gaps and connecting threads of style across the world with unmatched pace and reach.

5.1. From Runway to the Reel

Several factors are in play as fashion collides with the digital universe, the most prominent being the phenomenal speed of dissemination. In the traditional model, fashion trends emerged from the bi-annual Fashion Weeks in globally recognized fashion capitals like Paris, Milan, or New York. These trends, initially only accessible to the press, select buyers, and elite individuals, would take months to filter down into mainstream retail. Instagram, however, has become a game changer in this arena. A picture or a video taken live from the runway show can be uploaded onto this platform within seconds, breaking down the barriers that once held trends hostage to a seasonal calendar.

5.2. The Democratization of Fashion

Arguably the most significant transformation born from the interplay between Instagram and the fashion industry is the democratization of fashion. By virtue of its widespread accessibility, Instagram has given voice and visibility to style connoisseurs typically outside the hallowed halls of high fashion. As more voices define what 'fashion' is, long-standing norms of exclusivity and elitism are being leveled. Independent designers and creators now have the power to step into the limelight, often leading the way in setting new trends.

5.3. The Influencer Economy and Fashion Dissemination

The rise of influencers and bloggers on Instagram is another critical facet of this digital revolution in fashion trend dissemination. Endowed with enormous followings, these social media influencers use Instagram as the primary platform for showcasing their personal style. Over time, they have garnered a reputation for being trendsetters, with their posts and stories influencing their followers' fashion choices significantly. Consequently, fashion houses and brands have begun to collaborate with these influencers and bloggers, leveraging their reach and authenticity to complement their traditional marketing efforts.

5.4. The Visual Appeal of Instagram: A Perfect Match for Fashion

Another pivotal aspect of this digital revolution is Instagram's visual-oriented platform. Fashion, intrinsically linked to imagery, finds a perfect home in Instagram, which prioritizes high-quality visuals and engaging aesthetics. Therefore, it's not surprising that the fashion community — amateurs, professionals, retailers, and everyone in between — have embraced Instagram as their platform of choice, using vibrant posts and catchy hashtags to curate an audience and build a brand, be it personal or corporate.

5.5. The Story Feature: Bringing Behind-the-Scenes to the Forefront

One of the most innovative elements of Instagram, the 'story' feature, has also been instrumental in transforming the way high fashion experiences are shared with the masses. These ephemeral moments, which vanish after 24 hours, allow brands to shed light on the behind-the-scenes reality of fashion shows and previews. The result has been a greater connection between brands and their consumers, with transparency and authenticity emerging as significant factors that influence consumer-buying behaviors.

5.6. Challenges: The Flip Side of Digitization

However, the arrival of Instagram and the subsequent digital revolution in fashion is not without its trials. As information is disseminated faster, the fashion cycle's accelerated pace has led to increased pressure on designers and fashion houses to continually produce fresh, innovative collections. There have also been discussions surrounding overconsumption, fast fashion, and sustainability issues, triggered by the relentless churn of trends Instagram promotes.

In sum, the impact of Instagram and the digital revolution on the fashion world has been far-reaching and transformative. The path from catwalk to Instagram post, once long and winding, has been smoothed out and shortened, creating a new dynamic between fashion creators and consumers. While the challenges arising from this shift are considerable, they also present an opportunity for the fashion industry to adapt and evolve. The future of fashion is undeniably digital and integrated, using Instagram as a global runway for the latest trends.

Chapter 6. Hashtags and Styles: Social Media Influencing Trends

An undeniable catalyst of stylistic evolution in the age of digital disruption, social media continues to revolutionize the fashion realm, indelibly altering its paradigm. The synthesis of hashtags and styles has created a novel form of a conceptual thread, weaving a vibrant tapestry of trends across the social media landscape. The ubiquitous, instantaneous and borderless nature of social media communication has exponentially amplified the influence of fashion trends, subverting the traditional gates of fashion dissemination and democratizing style expression.

6.1. The Power of Hashtags

The simplicity and efficacy of hashtags unravel an exciting chronicle of their transformative impact on fashion trends. Consider them the hidden architects in the sprawling metropolis of social media. Hashtags, represented by the # symbol, serve as an efficient indexing mechanism on various social media platforms, most notably Instagram and Twitter. They bring together disparate posts that share common thematic content, enabling users to navigate the digital space easily and discover new content aligned with their interests. A single keyword or phrase, preceded by a hashtag, holds the power to congregate an inclusive array of responses, prompting multiple interpretations and applications. Unlike the seasoned fashion critics and Consumer behaviour, the ubiquitous hashtag has become a democratic tool for trendsetting and style evolution.

6.2. The Democratization of Fashion Trends

In the erstwhile era, fashion trends were primarily propagated top-down, spearheaded by distinguished designers and fashion tycoons. However, social media, with hashtags as cardinal components, has recalibrated this mechanism. It has fostered a democratization of trendsetting, where anyone with an internet connection and a knack for creativity can see their styles transforming into global fashion trends. This trend, termed as 'massclusivity', has replaced the traditional 'exclusivity' narrative of fashion. Bold patterns, eclectic colors, or vintage revivals may originate in small digital pockets but quickly gain virality due to the hashtag's digital ripple effect.

6.3. Fast Fashion and Social Media: A Rapidly Spinning Wheel

Fast fashion, another offspring of the digital age, primarily depends on breakneck trend production and consumption. Social media platforms, with their quick-paced nature, complement and support fast fashion's model perfectly. Hashtags swiftly encompass new styles spotted on runways, celebrities, or even in a local high street store's changing room and propel them into the digital mainstream, rendering the trend lifecycle even more ephemeral. The connection between fast fashion and social media, further augmented by hashtags, has created a cycle that mocks the clock speed, often at the jeopardy of sustainability.

6.4. The Influencer Factor: Driving Fashion Trends

The advent of 'Influencers' as the new-age fashion dictators has added another dimension to the social media fashion dynamic. These social media celebrities, possessing vast follower bases, wield enormous power in shaping and popularizing trends. Via strategic hashtag use, influencers can amplify their fashion ethos, turning even the most eccentric style choices into covetable trends. The collaboration between brands and influencers, utilizing hashtags for campaign promotion, has further strengthened this trend-driving mechanism.

6.5. Impact of User-generated Content on Fashion Trends

User-generated Content (UGC), another ground-breaking introduction of social media, brings fashion enthusiasts to the forefront of trendsetting. Everyday users share their unique style perspectives using hashtags, contributing to the ongoing global fashion dialogue. Encouraging UGC not only aligns brands with their customer base but also fuels fashion innovation, diversity, and inclusivity. The power of UGC, fired up by hashtags, thus facilitates a more engaged, more vibrant, and far more democratic fashion industry.

6.6. Challenges and Drawbacks

While the intersection of social media, hashtags and fashion seems harmonious and rewarding, it's not devoid of challenges. Questions around originality, sustainability, mental health implications, and digital divide have surfaced. Misuse of hashtags and issues regarding algorithmic bias further complicate the space. These potential pitfalls demand ongoing dialogue and introspection within the industry.

In the ever-morphing landscape of the fashion industry, the synergy between hashtags and styles has ushered in a new epoch of dynamic, democratized, and digitally-driven fashion trends. In tandem with industry evolvements, this relationship will continue to grow, shift, and reshape the stylistic zeitgeist, crafting a fascinating narrative for future fashion chronicles.

Chapter 7. The Role of Influencers and Bloggers in Fashion Trends

In the present digital era, influencers and bloggers have surfaced as the unsung heroes driving the fashion industry. Their carefully crafted blogs, artful Instagram photos, compelling YouTube videos, and Facebook posts swept in a new era, impacting the fashion industry significantly.

7.1. Influencers: Modern Muses of Fashion

The world of fashion, once dictated by fashion moguls and designers, has found new trendsetters in the form of influencers. Social media has provided a platform enabling the rise of influencers, not confined by geographical limits, a distinct departure from the traditional fashion industry.

These influencers, wielding followership that ranges from thousands to millions, command a potent influence. Every picture they post, every brand they endorse, and every style they showcase contribute significantly to setting fashion trends. With one click, they can send fashion enthusiasts into a stylish frenzy, creating demand where once none existed.

7.2. Bloggers: Creative Catalysts in the Industry

If influencers are the soldiers on the fashion front line, bloggers are the strategists charting the course. Diffusing in-depth analysis and meaningful narratives around fashion, bloggers are credited with catalyzing creativity within the industry. Their blogs serve as a bridge between consumers and fashion retailers, pouring insights into the latter's promotional strategies.

They emphasize fashion's fleeting nature while also foregrounding its cyclic characteristic. Older styles find revival in fresh narratives weaved by bloggers, ensuring that no element of the dynamic fashion domain is broadly left untouched.

7.3. Leverage of Loyal Followership

Influencers and bloggers share a profound, intimate relationship with their followers. Their popularity stems not from their celebrity status, but from the trust and credibility they have fostered over time. Each repost, like, share, or saved post in their favor is a testament to their significant reach and impact value.

When such influencers or bloggers feature fashion trends, their followers are inclined to adopt them, leading to micro-trends' formation, eventually snowballing into widespread popularity.

7.4. A Digital Window Display: In-App Shopping Trends

Influencers and bloggers have unlocked a newer dimension to fashion marketing by shrewdly employing social media's in-app shopping feature. The Instagram Shop or the Facebook Marketplace enables followers directly to purchase the outfit or accessory detailed in the posts.

Such accessibility, combined with instant visibility, has dramatically accelerated the conversion of fashion trends. It reduces the time that usually elapses between a product's display, its adoption, and, subsequently, its viral spread.

7.5. Social Proofing and Validation

In a society where information overload is the norm, influencers and bloggers often serve as guides, providing a direction to the curious yet confused fashion enthusiasts. Their endorsements deliver social proofing, and their follower-base is a validation of their credibility.

7.6. Rise of Micro-influencers

While influencers with millions of followers have substantial reach, the trend towards credibility and relatability has fueled the rise of micro-influencers. These influencers may have fewer followers; however, their direct engagement often leaves a more significant mark, influencing fashion trends at a grassroot level.

7.7. The Landscape of Influencer Marketing and Blogger Engagement

Brands are recognizing this shift in power, and the marketing budget allotted to influencers and bloggers showcases this. Influencer marketing is projected to be a 15 billion dollar industry by 2022. With collaborations, unique promotional codes, and affiliate marketing, fashion trends have found a new launchpad, bypassing traditional advertising networks.

7.8. Fashion's Future: From Follower to Trendsetter

The increased democratization of fashion trends by influencers and bloggers is shifting the industry from a monologue to a dialogue. Fashion conversation is no longer a one-way street, and this interactivity marks the backbone of the next wave in fashion.

Collaboration is the future, and influencers and bloggers are here to guide the path.

Chapter 8. Case Studies: Successes and Failures of Fashion Social Media Campaigns

Worlds of fashion and social media are intertwined to an extraordinary extent in the digital age, redefining how the industry operates and impacts its audience. This mutual evolution brings various examples of successes and failures, as fashion brands explore the uncharted digital landscape, trying to appeal to their audience using different methods, platforms, and strategies. This chapter will dive deep into the riveting and informative tales, providing insightful examples of how this symbiotic relationship has unfolded, for better or worse.

8.1. The Tale of Successful Campaigns

The realm of fashion brims with fantastic examples of successfully executed social media campaigns. These stories encapsulate the innovative and creative part of the industry, highlighting its ability to use social platforms to engage, attract, and most importantly, communicate with audiences around the media-littered globe.

8.1.1. Burberry's Art of the Trench Campaign

Burberry's pivotal 'Art of the Trench' campaign was a revolutionary leap when it was first unveiled in 2009, right at the dawn of social media's ascent. This campaign invited users to upload pictures of themselves on a microsite wearing Burberry's iconic trench coat. This cleverly designed user-generated content strategy allowed

Burberry not only to engage its customers but also feature real people in their products, creating a sense of community and relatability. This effort boosted the brand's online visibility and illustrated the impactful method of involving audiences in the storytelling process.

8.1.2. Dior's #DiorLoveChain Instagram Campaign

On a similar note, Dior's #DiorLoveChain campaign proved another successful instance of fostering community via social storytelling. Launched on Instagram, the campaign asked participants to respond to 'And You, What Would You Do For Love?' posting videos and tagging friends to continue the conversation. For each post featuring the hashtag #DiorLoveChain, Dior pledged to donate $1 to international charity WE Charity that supports education for young girls in Kenya. By encouraging users to share their take on an engaging topic, Dior successfully sparked mass conversation and goodwill, amplifying brand communication.

8.2. The Failed Fashion Endeavors

However, the digital landscape is not only filled with roses but also thorns. Not all attempts to navigate through this area have been successful, and instances of failed campaigns offer perhaps equally beneficial insights into the ethics and nuances of effective digital communication.

8.2.1. Swedish Brand H&M's Misplaced Advert

An unfortunate misstep was made by Swedish retail giant H&M in 2018, when they published an image of a young Black child modeling a hoodie emblazoned with the phrase 'coolest monkey in the jungle.' This choice of imagery triggered widespread backlash, criticized globally for its racial insensitivity. Owing to the immediate and omnipresent nature of social media, this blunder was quickly circulated, resulting in a mass boycott and loss of influencers and collaborators for the brand. This incident underscored the need to consider cultural and racial sensitivities, especially given the global reach social media affords.

8.2.2. Snap Inc.'s Offensive Rihanna Ad

Snap Inc., the parent company of Snapchat, faced significant criticism in 2018 for running an ad for a game called 'Would You Rather?' which posed the question, "Would you rather slap Rihanna or punch Chris Brown?" The ad, seen as making light of domestic violence (given Rihanna's history), sparked immediate backlash, leading to Snapchat's public apology and the removal of the ad. Rihanna's very public condemnation of the app resulted in a significant drop in Snapchat's stock price. This serves as a stark reminder of the responsibility social media platforms and those advertising on them have to ensure their content respects their audience's sensibilities.

8.3. The Lessons to Learn

Social media serves as a mirror for the fashion industry, reflecting the triumphs as well as the pitfalls. The remarkable success stories demonstrate the power of innovative thinking, customer engagement, and socially inclusive narratives. However, the failures underscore the necessity for sensitivity to a global audience's diverse cultural, racial, and personal norms. Adapting to these three key elements, brands can harness social media's full potential, contributing to the evolution of fashion industry's digital narrative. These captivating tales provide a snapshot of a dynamic landscape, making a persuasive case for the significance of social media in shaping the future of fashion. This study provokes reflection, invites participation, and illuminates the pathway that leads to the much-anticipated next chapter of this intriguing saga.

Chapter 9. Emerging Trends: TikTok and Fashion's Future

One cannot delve into the elaborate tapestry of technological synergy within the fashion industry without dedicating considerable commentary to the groundbreaking phenomenon of TikTok. From playful dance challenges to bold looks and unpredictable trends, the popular short video platform has shown the world that there's more to fashion than meets the eye. Purposefully interspersed with expert opinion, in-depth analysis, engaging narratives, and illustrative examples, the following section continually unravels the immense potential and idiosyncrasy of TikTok's future in fashion.

9.1. The Emergence of TikTok as a Fashion Powerhouse

The world became apprised of the force that TikTok is within the fashion industry, as it moved from offering whimsical filters and quirky trends to becoming a dynamic, disruptive alter-ego of the traditionally steadfast runway. New York, Paris, Milan, and London may have been the erstwhile meccas of fashion, but the needle has shifted, and eyeshadow-deep exploration reveals the power in 15-second clips reverberating from teenaged bedrooms around the global village. No longer confined to professional studios, fashion has taken a revolutionary leap, shifting from top-down industry declarations to a more democratic, participative, and broad-based interpretation of style.

9.2. Spotlighting Micro trends

TikTok is the perfect environment for 'micro-trends' – new fashion stylings that gain rapid popularity, only to fade as swiftly as they emerged. From tie-dye shirts, vibrant Bella Hadid-inspired bandanas to a sudden resurgence of DIY painted jeans, TikTok users are breathing life into a carousel of trends that traditional mediums can't keep stride with. These micro-trends, many borne out of both whim and necessity, echo the rapid, viral nature of TikTok itself, where the spotlight shines bright but fleetingly, forever hunting the 'next big thing'.

9.3. The Influence of TikTok on Major Fashion Brands

Fashion conglomerates are taking heed, recognising that there's a seismic shift occurring in how style is disseminated and embraced. Labels such as Gucci, Dior and Balenciaga are no strangers to the alluring world of TikTok, developing viral challenges and partnering with prominent content creators. They're leaning into the frenzied pace of the platform, bypassing conventional marketing methods in favour of the democratised, fast-paced, and inherently interactive nature of TikTok. Such collaborations mark a paradigm shift in marketing strategy, illustrating brands' willingness to meet consumers on their turf with open arms.

9.4. Disrupting Business As Usual

On TikTok, everyone is a potential influencer. Regular users who sport a notable style can inadvertently spark a trend, leading to sold-out items and explosive brand recognition. Even more intriguing, some TikTok personalities have designed entire capsule collections purely from creating style-related viral content. The platform not only provides a hotbed for creating trends but also for commerce. Companies can leverage linking functionality to guide viewers directly to their online outlets, ensuring a quick and seamless transition from viewer to consumer.

9.5. TikTok's Promise of a Transformative Future

TikTok is not any other digital platform; it's a vibrant melting pot of creativity and innovation where trends are born, nurtured from novelty to virality, and sometimes, extinguished. Its success lies in its community-driven approach, a mantra that inherently rejects hierarchy, injecting a fresh perspective into the fashion industry. With more fashion brands leveraging TikTok's interactive potential and more consumers demanding personalized experiences, the platform presents an exciting roadmap for the future.

In the labyrinth of social media's impact on fashion, TikTok emerges as an unexpected hero — a beacon of change and a trailblazer, perfectly attuned to the rhythm of the digital revolution. The possibilities that lie in wait fascinate industry leaders and casual observers alike, promising a thrilling, uncompromising journey into an even more interactive and inclusive fashion future. This section paints a comprehensive picture of the immense potential of TikTok's role in fashion's future, undeniably unfolding a captivating narrative of the ongoing interplay between fashion and digital technology.

Chapter 10. The Impact of Social Critique via Social Media on the Fashion Industry

In seminal moments of reflection, social media plays a crucial role in socio-cultural critique, with the fashion industry often being the center of focus. Platforms like Twitter, Facebook, Instagram have become significant channels through which ordinary individuals can express unsatisfied sentiments, scrutinize trends and norms, comment on the fashion industry's impacts on society, and demand change. This, in turn, has a considerable impact on brands, designers, influencers, and the fashion industry as a whole.

10.1. The Power of Social Media Critique

These critiques span various facets of the fashion industry, including but not limited to labor practices, sustainability, inclusivity, and representation. They capacitate the democratization of expressive voices, allowing almost anyone to be a critic with enough influence to command the attention of fashion houses. With the proliferation of hashtags, trending topics, and viral challenges, dissent and demand for change spread faster than ever before. The mechanics of these digital platforms often amplify these critiques beyond immediate networks, creating ripple effects that cause serious reverberations in the fashion industry. They can force brands to be accountable, lead to policy changes, influence design directions, and shift public perception, making social media critique a powerful tool in shaping the industry's landscape.

10.2. Impact on Labor Practices

Child labor, low-wage labor, and inhumane working conditions in the fast-fashion industry have been bared through starkly distressing social media posts. Revelations coupled with resistance against unethical practices have put significant pressure on brands resorting to such means, encouraging them to implement more ethical manufacturing, procurement, and selling practices. A notable example includes the response to the #PayUp campaign, which aimed to make fashion brands accountable for honoring their orders after the onset of the COVID-19 pandemic, leading brands like H&M and Zara to commit to doing so.

10.3. Impact on Sustainability

The fashion industry is among the world's top polluters, with fast fashion being a prime culprit. Social media critique has been instrumental in dragging this reality into the limelight, making consumers more informed about the ecological implications of their purchasing decisions. It's pushing brands towards a more sustainable model of production, notably so with the viral #WhoMadeMyClothes campaign after the Rana Plaza disaster, which both drew attention to labor issues and environmental sustainability.

10.4. Impact on Inclusivity and Representation

The persistent homogenous representation in the fashion industry has been constantly challenged via social media feeds. Criticisms on the lack of diversity in body types, age, race, and gender on runways and advertisements have pushed fashion campaigns to be more inclusive. In 2020, several brands faced backlash for their absence of diversity, with users boycotting and calling others to do the same until they saw changes, highlighting the tangible implications of social critique.

10.5. The Role of Cancel Culture

While social criticism plays an essential role in fostering change, it often catalyzes 'cancel culture'. This phenomenon refers to the public shaming and boycott of individuals or brands that are perceived to have done something offensive. While 'cancel culture' can ensure accountability, it can also eschew constructive dialogue and rehabilitation, leading to intensified polarization.

10.6. Harnessing Social Critique: The Way Forward

A crucial element for the fashion industry lies in harnessing the power of social critique. Fashion brands can lean into these conversations, view criticisms as opportunities for growth, make amends where necessary, and drive the change demanded by their consumer base. Brands that listen, respond, and adapt to their customers' demands are well-positioned to build trust and thrive in this constantly evolving landscape. However, this necessitates transparency, sincerity in addressing grievances, and a commitment to implementing real change.

In conclusion, the impact of social critique via social media on the fashion industry is multifold and powerful. It holds the industry accountable and democratizes fashion critique, leading brands to rethink, redesign, and reimagine their policies, practices, and representations. While it presents challenges, it also offers a path forward for the industry to be more ethical, responsible, inclusive, and sustainable, aligning more authentically with the values of the present-day consumers they seek to serve. This incredible synergy of critique and change is defining a new era for the fashion industry.

Chapter 11. Path Forward: Harnessing Social Media for the Next Fashion Frontier

As we embark on the uncharted waters of the future, continuously treading along the overlapping borderlines of fashion and technology, it becomes paramount to map out a trajectory. We're commencing upon a pioneering journey, harnessing the avant-garde power of social media for the upcoming fashion frontier.

11.1. To Infinity and Beyond: The Blossoming Synergy

Striding across the runway of reality straddled between concrete and code, the fashion industry finds itself at the helm, steering the ship of social media engagement with a compass calibrated by creativity. Given the digital renaissance influencing our world, we cannot merely predict - but must strategically plan - the path forward. Privacy will play a defining role, with stricter data laws potentially reshaping the way fashion houses converse through the medium of social media. Streamlining communication between brand and consumers whilst complying with privacy laws will require innovation and adjustment.

11.2. Social Media: A Catalyst for Circular Fashion

Simultaneously, as climate change concerns rise above the pithy veneer of environmentalist rhetoric, expect social media to catalyze the transition towards circular fashion. Concepts of sustainability and recycling will not just penetrate, but pervade our feeds. Brands will harness the momentum of green hashtags, ingraining them in their product lines and brand identities. In turn, social media algorithms will promote eco-conscious brands, impacting the cycle of life for fashion.

11.3. Influencers: The New Fashion Mavens

No discussion about social media and fashion's forward trajectory is complete without addressing the influencers who comprise this digital domain. Their metamorphosis from facilitators to decision-makers heralds a new era where the industry will increasingly rely on them. They are the new-age fashion mavens whose choices could dictate the styles en vogue and the pace of trend turnover. Massive followerships, empowered by the collective might of social media likes and shares, might secure them unprecedented influence over the industry's direction.

11.4. Virtual Trend-Setting: New Vogue in the Virtual World

Drawing inspiration from its sociotechnical counterpart, the fashion industry is likely to embrace virtual avatars and augmented reality (AR) further. Virtual showrooms and fitting rooms are just the beginning; we predict the advent of virtual influencers, digital clothing lines, and advanced AR filters emphasized on rendering realistic representations. Social media will be the bridge connecting this alternate world with reality, making digital fashion trends and experiences seamlessly blend into our physical lives.

11.5. Pioneering Interactive Shopping: From Impressions to Purchases

The next frontier also eyes a future where social media evolves from being a marketing platform to becoming a direct sales channel. Shoppable posts, already on the rise, will experience a tremendous boost. The integration of AI and machine learning can supercharge this transformation, promising a future where chatbots not only take size and color preferences but also check out and process payments, all within the confines of our favorite social media app.

11.6. Critique Driven Improvements: Social Media as a Tool for Change

Lastly, the amplifying magnitude of social critique via social media will compel the industry to improve its practices. While this has been a part of the discourse, it's likely to thrust into the limelight. From ethical sourcing to fair-wage practices, social media will become a powerful tool to create more transparency and resultant enhancements.

In conclusion, social media has woven itself into the stitching of the fashion industry's future, promising a delightful panorama of unprecedented progress. As we transcend traditional boundaries and embrace the digital frontier, this immersive symbiosis ensures the fashion industry's next wave will be shaped by the undulating currents of social media's limitless potential. As this era unfolds, we remain on standby, ready to bear witness to the fashion revolution that emanates from our very own screens. With bated breath, we anticipate the dawn of this new day as the cybernetic threads of the

World Wide Web intertwine with the fine fabric of fashion, forever altering its pattern. Treading this path, we must remember that while the road forward is unwritten, the potential is infinite – limited only by the scope of our imaginative ingenuity. Together, the fashion industry and social media stand at the precipice of an extraordinary new era, and the journey forward promises to be as glittering as it will be groundbreaking.